THE
PASSIONATE
LIFE

BIBLE STUDY SERIES

THE
Psalms
42–72
POETRY ON FIRE

Book 2

12-WEEK STUDY GUIDE

BroadStreet
PUBLISHING

BroadStreet Publishing Group, LLC
Racine, Wisconsin, USA
BroadStreetPublishing.com

Passionate Life Bible Study
The Psalms 42–72: POETRY ON FIRE BOOK 2
12-WEEK STUDY GUIDE

Copyright © 2016 The Passion Translation®

Edited by Jeremy Bouma

ISBN-13: 978-1-4245-5341-9 (soft cover)
ISBN-13: 978-1-4245-5342-6 (e-book)

Cover design by Garborg Design at GarborgDesign.com
Typesetting by Katherine Lloyd at theDESKonline.com

Printed in the United States of America

16 17 18 19 20 5 4 3 2 1

Contents

Using This Passionate Life Bible Study

The psalmist declares, "Truth's shining light guides me in my choices and decisions; the revelation of your Word makes my pathway clear" (Psalm 119:105).

This verse forms the foundation of the Passionate Life Bible Study series. Not only do we want to kindle within you a deep, burning passion for God and his Word, but we also want to let the Word's light blaze a bright path before you to help you make truth-filled choices and decisions, while encountering the heart of God along the way.

God longs to have his Word expressed in a way that would unlock the passion of his heart. Inspired by The Passion Translation but usable with any other Bible translation, this is a heart-level Bible study, from the passion of God's heart to the passion of your heart. Our goal is to trigger inside you an overwhelming response to the truth of the Bible, unfiltered by religious jargon.

DISCOVER. EXPLORE. EXPERIENCE. SHARE.

Each of the following lessons is divided into four sections: *Discover the Heart of God*; *Explore the Heart of God*; *Experience the Heart of God*; and *Share the Heart of God*. They are meant to guide your study of the truth of God's Word, while drawing you closer and deeper into his passionate heart for you and your world.

The *Discover* section is designed to help you make observations about the reading. Every lesson opens with the same three questions: What did you notice, perhaps for the first time? What questions do you have? And, what did you learn about the heart of God? There are no right answers here! They are meant to jump-start your journey into God's truth by bringing to the surface your initial impressions about the passage. The other questions help draw your attention to specific points the author wrote and discover the truths God is conveying.

Explore takes you deeper into God's Word by inviting you to think more critically and explain what the passage is saying. Often there is some extra information to highlight and clarify certain aspects of the passage, while inviting you to make connections. Don't worry if the answers aren't immediately apparent. Sometimes you may need to dig a little deeper or take a little more time to think. You'll be grateful you did, because you will have tapped into God's revelation-light in greater measure!

Experience is meant to help you do just that: experience God's heart for you personally. It will help you live out God's Word by applying it to your unique life situation. Each question in this section is designed to bring the Bible into your world in fresh, exciting, and relevant ways. At the end of this section, you will have a better idea of how to make choices and decisions that please God, while walking through life on clear paths bathed in the light of his revelation!

The final section is *Share*. God's Word isn't meant to be merely studied or memorized; it's meant to be shared with other people—both through living and telling. This section helps you understand how the reading relates to growing closer to others, to enriching your fellowship and relationship with your world. It also helps you listen to the stories of those around you, so you can bridge Jesus' story with their stories.

SUGGESTIONS FOR INDIVIDUAL STUDY

Reading and studying the Bible is an exciting journey! Yet it isn't like studying for that American history, calculus, or chemistry class back in the day, where the goal was just fact gathering and memorizing information. Instead, think of this journey more like reading your favorite novel—where the purpose is encountering the heart and mind of the author through its characters and conflict, plot points, and prose.

This study is designed to help you encounter the heart of God and let his Word to you reach deep down into your very soul—all so you can live and enjoy the life he intends for you. And like with any journey, a number of practices will help you along the way:

1. Begin your lesson time in prayer, asking God to open up his Word to you in new ways, expose areas of your heart that need teaching and healing, and correct any area in which you're living contrary to his desires for your life.

2. Read the opening section to gain an understanding of the major themes of the reading and ideas for each lesson.

3. Read through the Scripture passage once, underlining or noting in your Bible anything that stands out to you. Reread the passage again, keeping in mind these three questions: What did you notice, perhaps for the first time? What questions do you have? What did you learn about the heart of God?

4. Write your answers to the questions in this Bible study guide or another place of choice. Take your time and don't get discouraged if you're unsure of an answer. If you do get stuck, first ask God to reveal his Word to you and guide you in his truth. And then, either wait until your small group time or ask your pastor or another teacher for help.

5. Use the end of the lesson to focus your time of prayer, thanking and praising God for the truth of his Word, for what he has revealed to you, and for how he has impacted your daily life.

SUGGESTIONS FOR SMALL GROUP STUDY

Think of your small group more like a book club rather than a group studying for a college class. The point isn't to memorize a list of facts and score points for right answers. The goal is to understand God's Word for you and your community in greater measure, while encountering his heart along the way. A number of practices will also help your group as you journey together:

1. Group studies usually go better when everyone is prepared to participate. The best way to prepare is to come having read the lesson's Scripture reading beforehand. Following the suggestions in each individual study will enrich your time as a community as well.

2. Before you begin the study, your group should nominate a leader to guide the discussion. While this person should work through the questions beforehand, his or her main job isn't to lecture, but to help move the conversation along by asking the lesson questions and facilitating the discussion.

3. This study is meant to be a community affair where everyone shares. Be sure to listen well, contribute where you feel led, and try not to dominate the conversation.

4. The number one rule for community interaction is: nothing is off-limits! No question is too dumb; no answer is out of bounds. While many questions in this study have "right" answers, most are designed to push you and your friends to explore the passage more deeply and understand what it means for daily living.

5. Finally, be ready for God to reveal himself through the passage being discussed and through the discussion that arises out of the group he's put together. Pray that he would reveal his heart and revelation-light to you all in deeper ways. And be open to being challenged, corrected, and changed.

Again, we pray and trust that this Bible study will kindle in you a burning, passionate desire for God and his heart, while impacting your life for years to come. May it open wide the storehouse of heaven's revelation-light. May it reveal new and greater insights into the mysteries of God and the kingdom-realm life he has for you. And may you encounter the heart of God in more fresh and relevant ways than you ever thought possible!

Introduction to the Exodus Psalms
Book 2

Every emotion of the heart is reflected in the Psalms with words that express our deepest and strongest feelings. They provide comfort and joy, leading us to the place where worship flows. *Poetry on Fire* is divided into five books, mirroring the five books of Moses that form the first few books of the Old Testament. Together they convey the depth of our longings and fears, joys and celebrations, becoming a mirror to the heart of God's people in our quest to experience God's presence.

Book Two is known as the Exodus Psalms. Like the ancient Hebrew book of Exodus itself, which chronicles Israel's deliverance out of oppression, these psalms lament our suffering and long for similar redemption. Many poems are cries to God for help; they ask him to wake up and do something about our trials and trouble. Others wonder if God has forgotten his people in the midst of their pain and problems. Still other psalms cry for revival and renewal, praying from a place of weariness and ache. Then there are the poems that praise God for his faithfulness, protection, and grace—leading to faith and trust.

We've designed this study to help you explore these praises and prayers placed inside poems that spill out of a fiery, passionate heart. May the study of this poetry on fire free you to become a passionate, sincere worshiper, and to experience the heart of God anew in faith and worship.

Lesson 1

Never Fear, God Is on Your Side!

PSALMS 42–43, 46

So we will never fear even if every structure of support were to crumble away! We will not fear even when the earth quakes and shakes, moving mountains and casting them into the sea! For the raging roar of stormy winds and crashing waves cannot erode our faith in you.
(Psalm 46:2-3)

Book Two of Psalms is known as the Exodus Psalms. Like the ancient Hebrew book itself, which chronicles the exodus of Israel out of oppression and into deliverance, these psalms lament our suffering and long for deliverance.

The book opens with the psalmist crying for revival, a plea that his own soul's thirst for God would be quenched. The psalmist is like a parched deer longing for a brook of bliss to find relief from his depression and despair. This cry is similar to what the children of Israel themselves would have offered to God while in Egypt. The psalmist also beseeches the Lord to plead his case, to deliver him from the hands of his accusers, and to pour into him his light and guidance.

Along his path of lamentation and beseeching, the psalmist reminds us of a singular truth: we have no need to fear, because God is on our side. Even if the earth were to quake and shake and the mountains were to slide into the ocean, even in the midst of raging and storming seas, there's no reason to fear—because we discover that God is our refuge, our strength. He's a proven help in times of trouble.

Discover the Heart of God

- After reading Psalms 42, 43, and 46, what did you notice, perhaps for the first time? What questions do you have? What did you learn about the heart of God?

- As the psalmist of Psalm 42 spoke over his heartbroken soul, what did he remember? What did the psalmist ask his soul? What did he tell himself to do with it?

- What did the psalmist of Psalm 43 want God to do for him? What did God mean to the psalmist? What would the psalmist do in response?

- Even if his structures of support were to crumble away, and even through earthquakes, stormy winds, and crashing waves, what did the psalmist of Psalm 46 say he wouldn't do?

- What are the "breathtaking wonders of our God" (46:8–9)? What has the mighty Lord of Angel-Armies done for us?

- What does the Lord tell us to do in Psalm 46? Why?

Explore the Heart of God

- While the opening of Psalm 42 is sometimes sung as a praise song, it's actually a song of lament. What was the psalmist lamenting? Why did he urge his soul to "remember," and why is this act of remembering so important to experiencing the heart of God?

- Why could the psalmist say to his soul, "Don't be discouraged. Don't be disturbed. For I know my God will break through for me" in Psalms 42—and then say something similar in Psalm 43?

- What does it tell us about the character and heart of God that he is "a safe and powerful place to find refuge" and "a proven help in time of trouble" (46:1)?

- In what way does the city of God-Most-High "bring joy and delight to his people" (46:4)? How does the God of Jacob fight for us?

- Why can we be still and know that God is God? Why can you "surrender your anxiety! Be silent and stop your striving" (46:10)? What will happen when we do?

Experience the Heart of God

- When have you felt like a deer thirsting, panting, and longing for the Living God?

- The next time you cry out for help, how might the act of remembering God's faithfulness and your experience of his joy help you experience the heart of God?

- If you are depressed and downcast, meditate on the refrain from Psalms 42 and 43: "Don't be discouraged. Don't be disturbed. For I know my God will break through for me."

- Do you truly believe that God is "where [your] strength comes from and [your] Protector" (43:2)? How might it look for you to fully rest in that reality?

- In what ways has God proven to you that he is "a powerful place to find refuge" in times of trouble? How has he been "more than enough and always available" (46:1) whenever you've needed him?

- God promises that he is our source of joy and delight, that he is with us, and that he will fight for us. How would you like him to be all three for you today? Now spend time asking him to do so.

Share the Heart of God

- Who do you know whose soul "thirsts, pants, and longs for the living God" (Psalm 42:2)? How might it look to encourage them by sharing the heart of God?

- Why might sharing 42:11 and 43:5 with someone you know be a great way to share the heart of God? Commit to doing that this week.

• Do you show people with your life that God is your strength and protector when times get tough? How might doing so be crucial to sharing the heart of God?

• Our world is full of trouble, and fear lurks around every corner. How might sharing Psalm 46 with those you know be a way to share the heart of God?

• Who do you know who needs a "safe and powerful place to find refuge," who needs God to "bring joy and delight" and be on their side? Take time to pray that God would be this for them, but also share with them the heart of God found in Psalm 46.

CONSIDER THIS

Perhaps you feel like the Israelites at the start of Exodus: oppressed, parched, and distressed. Never fear! God is a safe and powerful refuge when life quakes and shakes. He is a proven help in times of trouble when the world around you surges and storms. So don't be discouraged or disturbed. God will break through for you, for he is on your side!

Lesson 2

———

Remember, Honor, and Serve the Lord Alone

PSALMS 44 AND 45

If we had forsaken your holy name, wouldn't you know it?
You'd be right in leaving us. If we had worshiped before
other gods, no one would blame you for punishing us.
God, you know our every heart-secret. You know we still want you!
(Psalm 44:20–21)

One consistent feature of Israel's story is how they consistently forsook their first love, Yahweh. Remember the golden calf they made shortly after being delivered from Egypt and brought into relationship with him? That wasn't the last of their foreign-god adultery either, and the Lord punished them for it.

Yet there were also times when God's people hadn't forsaken him and they still experienced suffering; they were faithful but it seemed like God wasn't. And surprisingly, the singers of Korah's clan confronted God about it. They revealed they hadn't forgotten him, hadn't broken covenant, hadn't betrayed him—not like before. Yet they'd been treated like slaughtered sheep, sold as slaves, despised and scorned. "So wake up, Lord God!" they demanded. "Why would you sleep when we're in trouble?" (44:23).

Today, from our psalms, we discover a few lessons that inform our suffering: sometimes it's not our fault; since God is sovereign over our lives, we can ask him about it; and not all suffering is positive. What's required of us through it all is that we remember what the Lord has done, honor and trust him, and live a blameless life by desiring him alone.

Discover the Heart of God

- After reading Psalms 44 and 45, what did you notice, perhaps for the first time? What questions do you have? What did you learn about the heart of God?

- In Psalm 44, what had the psalmist heard from his ancestors about what the Lord had done for his people?

- What had changed in the life of the psalmist and the people? List all of what the Lord was doing. What did the psalmist want God to do about it?

• In what way was the psalmist's heart in Psalm 45 stirred and "on fire, boiling over with passion" for the Lord (v. 1)? List some of what bubbled up within him.

• What did the psalmist instruct the "daughters" in Psalm 45 to do?

Explore the Heart of God

• What were all of the glorious miracles God had performed for his people that the psalmist had heard? List them.

• How did remembering what God had done for the ancient ancestors help the psalmist of Psalm 44 trust in God for victory?

- Psalm 44:9–22 explains that what Israel suffered wasn't because of sin. What does this tell us about some of what we suffer in this life? What does 44:23–26 tell us about the heart of God in response?

- Many believe Psalm 45 was the wedding song composed for Solomon when he married the princess of Egypt. But the language is so lofty and glorious that we see One greater than Solomon in its verses. This is a song of the wedding of Jesus and his Bride, the church. How does this expanded meaning deepen your understanding of the psalm and the heart of God?

- Given that one way we read Psalm 45 is as a love poem between Jesus and his Bride, what does 45:10–11 mean for our experience of the heart of God?

Experience the Heart of God

- What are all the glorious miracles of God you have heard about from those you know? How should they encourage your experience of the heart of God?

- Do you trust in the weapons of the world or only the Lord's "glorious name" and "awesome power" (44:5) for victory? Explain.

- Psalm 44:9–22 speaks of a time of faithfulness to God and also suffering. Have you ever experienced something similar? How did the Lord's unfailing love save you from that sorrow?

- In Psalm 45, the psalmist's heart was "on fire, boiling over with passion" for the Lord. What kind of lyrics are "bubbling up within [you] ... as a lovely poem to be sung for the King" (v. 1)?

• Read 45:10–11 again. In what ways do you, a "daughter" who is part of the Bride of Christ, need to "put behind you every attachment to the familiar, even those who once were close to you!" (v. 10)? In what ways do you need to "bow in reverence before him, for he is your Lord!" (v. 11)?

Share the Heart of God

• The psalmist of Psalm 44 seemed to trust God because of all the glorious miracles he'd heard about God doing for his people. What can you share about what God has done for you to share the heart of God with someone you know who is struggling?

• Do you know someone who is suffering despite their faithfulness? Spend time asking God to "arise, awake, and come to help us, O Lord" (44:26).

- What we say about God and how we praise him and his glory has great bearing on how we share the heart of God with others. How might the lyrics you sang about in the fourth question of the previous section help others share in the heart of God?

- Why is sharing the theme of 45:10–11 an important aspect of sharing the heart of God with those we know?

- The psalmist of Psalm 45 said, "I will make sure the fame of your name is honored in every generation as all the people praise you, giving you thanks forever and ever!" (v. 17). How might it look to follow the psalmist in doing the same in your world?

CONSIDER THIS

Though not all suffering is our fault, we should do all we can to make sure there's no blood on our hands by leading a blameless life. So boil over with passion for the King of kings alone. Join the daughters "and forget about your past. Put behind you every attachment to the familiar" (45:10) by remembering what the Lord has done and desiring no one but him!

Lesson 3

———

Our God Reigns!

PSALMS 47 AND 48

Our God reigns over every nation!
He reigns on his holy throne over all.
(Psalm 47:8)

If there's one thing the book of Exodus proves, it's that our God reigns. The Exodus Psalms found in today's lesson echo this profound, comforting truth.

At the time of Israel's oppression and suffering, Egypt was the largest, most powerful empire on the planet. They commanded the military might of chariots. Their land was the breadbasket of the surrounding area, lending to economic might. And Moses was supposed to come against this might and power to liberate and redeem God's oppressed people—a people who were the least mighty and powerful? No way! Yes way! Because our God reigns over every nation, even the might and power of Egypt. You know what? He still reigns; he is the king over all the earth.

Sometimes we need the reminder that all of the powers and might of this world can't compare to the Mighty Lord of Angel-Armies who is always on our side. That's what you'll discover and explore in this lesson. And what you'll praise him for afterward.

Discover the Heart of God

- After reading Psalms 47 and 48, what did you notice, perhaps for the first time? What questions do you have? What did you learn about the heart of God?

- What did the psalmist of Psalm 47 instruct us to do? Why?

- What had the Lord done for his people that required praise and worship? How does God respond to such praise?

- Over what does God reign? What belongs to him?

- How is Zion described in Psalm 48? How did kings respond when they saw her?

- What should the people of God recall as they worship the Lord? Why should people "rejoice with gladness" and "leap for joy" (48:11)?

Explore the Heart of God

- What does Psalm 47:1 tell us about the kind of praise and worship we should have? What about verse 6?

- What does it tell us about the heart of God that he conquers on our behalf and marks out our inheritance for us?

- What does it say about God that "the powers of earth are all his" (v. 7), that God "reigns over every nation" (v. 8)? Why should we "sing [our] celebration songs of highest praise" (v. 7) because of this reality?

- Why is the psalmist right that "there are so many reasons to describe God as wonderful! So many reasons to praise him with unlimited praise!" (48:1). List some reasons here.

- In Psalm 48, what is the psalmist saying about God's dwelling place—and God himself?

- When we worship, why should we "recall over and over [his] kindness to us and [his] unending love" (v. 9)?

Experience the Heart of God

- When you worship God, do you reflect the kind of worship in 47:1 and 6, a worship of never-ending celebration? How would such worship impact your experience of the heart of God? Explain.

- In what way is God the one who has conquered and provided an inheritance for you?

- The psalmist is right: "There are so many reasons to describe God as wonderful! So many reasons to praise him with unlimited praise!" (48:1). What are all the personal reasons that you'd describe God as wonderful?

- Why does it matter to your experience of the heart of God that the city of God is "safe and secure forever" (v. 8)?

- What does it mean to you and your experience of the heart of God that he "is our God, our great God forever. He will lead us onward until the end, through all time, beyond death, and into eternity!" (v. 14)?

Share the Heart of God

- Why is our never-ending celebration and joy of God so important to our sharing the heart of God?

- The psalmist writes that God is the one who conquers for us and marks out our inheritance. Why might this encourage those you know to share in the heart of God?

- Go back to the list you made for the third question in the last section. Choose one of those "so many reasons" to share the heart of God with people you know, to share with them the heart of God and help them see how wonderful he is.

- The psalmist of Psalm 48 tells us to "go and tell the coming generation of the care and compassion of our God" (v. 13). How might it look to follow the psalmist and share the heart of God with the coming generation you know?

CONSIDER THIS

There's a popular song that repeats our declaration as its chorus: "Our God reigns! Our God reigns! Our God reigns! Our God reigns!"[1] What comfort is found in these three simple words! Spend time meditating over them, repeating them to yourself. Then "sing and celebrate! Sing some more, celebrate some more! Sing your highest song of praise to our King!" (47:6). For our God reigns!

---

1   Leonard E. Smith, "Our God Reigns," New Jerusalem Music, 1974.

Lesson 4

———

"Faith," Don't "Fear"!

PSALMS 49, 50, AND 58

Honor me by trusting in me in your day of trouble.
Cry aloud to me, and I will be there to rescue you.
That is what I desire from you!
(Psalm 50:15)

F-E-A-R. What a tiny word. What a *big* word! Whether it's a news report on the latest unemployment figures or stock market dip, whether you get a message from your doctor's office or your estranged parent, whether your friend stabs you in the back or your family disowns you—fear and pain lurks around every corner.

And yet David invites us in this lesson to "faith" instead of "fear," discovering "there's no reason to fear when troubling times come" (Psalm 49:5). One reason is that those who persecute and cause so much trouble can't save themselves. There will be a day when "the brightest and best, along with the foolish and senseless" will die (v. 10). Another reason is God is the Mighty One, a God of justice who will sweep away the wicked. Here's the best reason of all: God will redeem our soul, raising us up from the power of death and taking us to be his bride.

You'll also discover that, while we don't have to "fear," we do have to

32

"faith." God invites us to actively assume a posture of faith to honor him. When we do, we will celebrate in triumph.

Discover the Heart of God

- After reading Psalms 49, 50, and 58, what did you notice, perhaps for the first time? What questions do you have? What did you learn about the heart of God?

- Who should listen to the psalmist's words in Psalm 49? What don't they have any reason to do when troubling times come, even when they're surrounded by wicked deceivers?

- What happens to "the brightest and best, along with the foolish and senseless"?

- What does God say to "all the people of the earth in every brilliant sunrise and every beautiful sunset" (50:1)? What does the mighty Lord do when he comes to earth? What does he say when he does?

- What of ours doesn't the Lord need? What does he desire instead?

Explore the Heart of God

- Why is there "no reason to fear when troubling times come, even when you're surrounded with problems and persecutors who chase at your heels" (49:5)? How might the "trust" in this verse be connected to not fearing?

- Read Psalm 49:10 again. What does it tell us about life? Why is chasing after wealth fruitless? Why don't you have to be "disturbed when you see the rich surround you with the 'glory' of their wealth on full display" (49:16)?

• Why does God bring his people to trial in Psalm 50? What have they done, or not done?

• What does it mean that the Lord doesn't need our "young bull or goats from [our] fields" (50:9)? Why not?

• What is the life that pleases God? Why does our trust honor him? What does this kind of life reveal about the heart of God?

• What does it mean that even from birth the wicked go astray? Why does David want God to break their fangs, shatter their teeth, and let them disappear and dissolve? Why is this a good thing to celebrate?

Experience the Heart of God

- When troubling times come and you're surrounded by problems, do you "fear" or "faith"? Explain. Do you honor the Lord by trusting in him in your day of trouble? Why or why not?

- How might it deepen your experience of the heart of God if you trusted in him to solve your problems—rather than trusting your treasures or other resources like the rich?

- Have you contemplated your own death, that you will die along with "the brightest and best, along with the foolish and senseless" (49:10)? How should verse 15 inform that contemplation and your experience of the heart of God?

- How would it look in your life to bring the sacrifice God desires by bringing him "your true and sincere thanks" and showing him "your gratitude" by keeping your promises to him (50:14)?

- Do you feel the same way about the wicked as David did in Psalm 58? Why or why not? How does it impact your experience of the heart of God to know that "'there is a God who judges the judges'; and 'there is a great reward in loving God!'" (v. 11)?

Share the Heart of God

- With whom can you share the heart-of-God news that "there's no reason to fear when troubling times come, even when you're surrounded with problems and persecutors who chase at your heels" (49:5)?

- Why is it so important to sharing the heart of God that "the brightest and best, along with the foolish and senseless, God sees that they all will die one day" (v. 10)?

- In Psalm 50, the Lord judges both the righteous and the wicked. What is it from this psalm that God might want to use you to communicate to those you know?

- For people who are far from God, the words of Psalm 50:22 are significant. Read them again. With whom can you share the heart of God to help them turn away from evil?

- How might it help those you know experience the heart of God to know "'there is a God who judges the judges'; and 'there is a great reward in loving God!'" (58:11)?

CONSIDER THIS

Have you ever considered that one way you honor the Lord is by trusting him? By having faith that he will come through for you and redeem you out from under whatever oppression you are experiencing? Do that right now: honor the Lord by crying out to him aloud in trust, "faithing" that he will be there to rescue you. For that is what he desires.

Lesson 5

———

Lord, Do Heart Surgery!

PSALMS 51, 52, AND 53

Purify my conscience! Make this leper clean again!
Wash me in your love until I am pure in heart. ... Start over
with me, and create a new, clean heart within me. Fill me with
pure thoughts and holy desires, ready to please you.
(Psalm 51:7, 10)

Sometimes we are oppressed by and suffer from forces on the outside. But sometimes the problem lies within; we're the ones that cause ourselves so much heartache and give ourselves so many headaches. That's because we have a heart problem, one that's been with us from birth.

David realized this after he had been "outed" for committing adultery with Bathsheba and then killing her husband, Uriah, to cover it up. He was so ashamed and was in so much pain and anguish because of his sin. The corruption of his sin had polluted his heart from birth—and he wanted the Lord to do something about it. David wanted the Lord to get inside, with the precision of a cardiologist, and teach him wisdom; purify him and make him clean; satisfy him with his goodness; and create within him a new, clean heart.

This lesson is for everyone; we're all called to listen up! Because as David revealed, "all have wandered astray, walking stubbornly toward evil" (53:3).

Discover the Heart of God

- After reading Psalms 51, 52, and 53, what did you notice, perhaps for the first time? What questions do you have? What did you learn about the heart of God?

- What did David want God to do with his sins? List them here. What was David's reaction to his sin? What did he know and feel about it? What did David want God to do with his heart? What did he want God to fill him with and restore him to? What would be the result?

- In Psalm 52, David asked the wicked a question; what was it?

- What did David say the wicked love? How will the Almighty respond? How about the godly?

- What does only the "withering soul" (53:1) say to himself? How are such people described in Psalm 53? How many people does God find who seek him? How many are good?

Explore the Heart of God

- What is the context of Psalm 51? How does that context connect to verses 3–4?

- What does Psalm 51 teach us about sin and also the heart of God in the midst of it? What does Psalm 51 reveal about how we should respond to our sin and God's forgiveness of it?

- How does God purify, satisfy, and "create a new, clean heart" within us (v. 10)?

• In what ways do the wicked boast in evil? How will God deal with them, especially in the end? Why are the righteous, like David, like a flourishing olive tree? What makes them flourish?

• Why is anyone who says, "There is no God" considered "corrupt and callous," "depraved and detestable," and "devoid of what is good" (53:1)?

• Why is the revelation-truth of 53:2–3 true? How similar or different is this from what our culture says about the nature and goodness of people?

Experience the Heart of God

• When have you prayed what David did in Psalm 51? Have you ever felt what David voiced in verses 2–5? What was that like?

- Is there anything you'd like the Lord to purify, cleanse, and wash you from? If so, spend time asking God to do that now. In what way would you like God to "create a new, clean heart within me. Fill me with pure thoughts and holy desires, ready to please you" (v. 10)?

- How should it impact your experience of the heart of God that he has delivered you fully from every sin?

- How does it make you feel to know the Almighty will strike down evil people forever?

- How have you witnessed the truth that "all have wandered astray, walking stubbornly toward evil. Not one is good; he can't even find one!" (53:3)? Do you ever find yourself praying what David did in verse 6 in the face of so much worldly wickedness? Explain.

Share the Heart of God

- Do you know anyone who feels ashamed and the sting of their sin? How might it look to share with them the heart of God found in Psalm 51?

- One of the results of our own forgiveness and being cleansed from sin is showing "to other guilty ones how loving and merciful" God is to them, so "they will find their way back home to [him], knowing that [he] will forgive them" (51:13). How would you like to show or share such love and mercy with those you know?

- How should 52:3 motivate us to share the heart of God with those we know who boast in evil?

- How might it look in your life to share the heart of God by "praising [the Lord] forever and giving [him] thanks!" (52:9)?

- Do you know anyone who says in their heart, "There is no God"? Take time to pray for them, that they would powerfully encounter and experience the heart of God to change their heart and mind.

CONSIDER THIS

Jesus reminded us that "what comes out of your mouth reveals the core of your heart. ... You will find living within an impure heart, evil ideas, murderous thoughts, adultery, sexual immorality, theft, lies, and slander. That's what pollutes a person" (Matthew 15:18–20). Take time to pray for the things that come out of your heart, that the Lord would purify your heart and renovate it!

Lesson 6

Lord, Defend Me from My Enemies!

PSALMS 54 AND 55

Come close to me and give me your answer.
Here I am, moaning and restless. I'm preoccupied with
the threats of my enemies and crushed by the pressure of
their opposition. They surround me with trouble and terror.
In their fury they rise up against me in an angry uproar.
(Psalm 55:2–3)

If last week's lesson was about our enemy on the inside—our trouble-some heart—this one is about our enemies on the outside. The ones who surround us with trouble and terror, who accuse us and attack us, and who try to bring us down and take us out.

David had been on the run from Saul. It wasn't because of anything he had done but because of Saul's jealous hatred. "Violent men have risen up against me," David explained, "heartless, ruthless men who care nothing about God—they seek to take my life" (54:3). Can you relate? Have you voiced this in exasperation before: "If only I could fly away from all of this!

If only I could run away to the place of rest and peace. I would run far away where no one could find me, escaping to a wilderness retreat" (55:6–7)?

If you have, then this lesson is for you! It's for those of us who are assaulted by enemies—human or not. It's for those of us who are crying out, "Lord, defend me from my enemies!" What we discover is how faithful God is when others are not.

Discover the Heart of God

- After reading Psalm 54 and 55, what did you notice, perhaps for the first time? What questions do you have? What did you learn about the heart of God?

- By what did David want to be delivered? What did David want God to do for him in Psalm 54? What had he become for David?

- What did David promise to offer the Lord? Why?

- What didn't David want the Lord to do while he cried out to him? What did he want him to do instead?

- Describe what David was feeling and experiencing in the midst of his threats and troubles in Psalm 55.

- What was all that David had learned through his betrayal?

Explore the Heart of God

- Psalm 54 describes itself as a song of derision, or mocking. It's a psalm for anyone who feels betrayed, rejected, and in a difficult situation with no one at their side. What does it reveal about the heart of God that he would give us such a psalm?

- In what way has God become our "divine Helper"? How does he uphold and sustain us? In what way will God "see to it that those who sow evil will reap evil" (54:5)?

- What does Psalm 55:1–7 tell us about the intense emotional reactions people experience in the face of threats and troubles? How does verse 8 answer them?

- What does Psalm 55, especially verse 17, teach us about prayer?

- Even though David was betrayed, he learned a number of lessons through it all. What do the lessons he learned in 55:22–23 reveal about the heart of God?

Experience the Heart of God

- How have you personally experienced and witnessed the sustaining reality of God's title "divine Helper"?

- Is it comforting to know that "God will see to it that those who sow evil will reap evil" and you will be "rescued from every trouble" (54:5, 7)?

- Have you ever been betrayed by a close friend, as David had been in Psalm 55? What was that like? How did it feel?

- When trouble comes and betrayal happens, how would it look in your life to do what David did—to pray every evening, morning, and waking hour?

- Read 55:22–23 again. How might resting in what David learned give you hope and deepen your experience of the heart of God?

Share the Heart of God

- Who is someone you know who needs saving and deliverance? How might Psalm 54 impact their experience of the heart of God? Now spend time asking the Lord to be their divine Helper, to uphold and sustain them.

- How might your worship of God in response to the Lord saving and rescuing you from every trouble be a way you can share the heart of God with those you know?

- Fear and dread overwhelm people in our world. What does Psalm 55 have in store for those you know to help them share in the heart of God?

- Do you know anyone who has been betrayed by someone close to them? How can you share the heart of God with them to reassure them that God's "measureless grace will strengthen" them (55:22)?

- In what way might placing your life's hope and trust in the Lord be an opportunity to share and show the heart of God with those you know?

CONSIDER THIS

If you've been betrayed, if you feel surrounded by enemies and assaulted on every side, take heart. God himself will hear you, the one enthroned through everlasting ages who is unchanging in his faithfulness. Hide yourself in your Shelter, for through him you are saved from every trouble. You will see the defeat of your enemies, and you will triumph over them. For he will put them in their place!

Lesson 7

———

Quiet and Confident, Trust and Praise

PSALMS 56, 57, AND 59

My heart, O God, is quiet and confident.
Now I can sing with passion your wonderful praises!
(Psalm 57:7)

Can your own heart claim such a status? That it's "quiet and confident" when life goes dark, that you can sing God's wonderful praises when hope fades?

That's exactly what David declared when his life spun out of control. He was on the run from Saul, whose heart had turned jealous with hatred. When he penned this song, David was hiding in a cave, having been on the run while trying to evade capture and certain death. Yet he wasn't chaotic and fearful. Quiet and confident was he.

During another time when David was surrounded by fierce foes, he echoed this heart status, saying not once but twice, "What harm could man do to me? With God on my side I will not be afraid of what comes" (Psalm 56:4). Later he declared, "The God of passionate love will meet with me. My God will empower me to rise in triumph over my foes" (59:10). Again, quiet and confident.

How could he say this? What would guide his heart into this kind of peace? Discover and explore the two words that led to this: *trust* and *praise.*

Discover the Heart of God

- After reading Psalms 56, 57, and 59, what did you notice, perhaps for the first time? What questions do you have? What did you learn about the heart of God?

- What did David do in Psalm 56, and how did he respond when he was afraid? List all the ways here.

- How were David's cruel critics treating him? Why did he want God to respond?

- Until his terrible trouble passed, what did David say he would do in Psalm 57? What would God do in response?

- In Psalm 59, what did David want God to do in response to his enemies?

- In Psalm 59, where did David recognize his strength was found? What would God do for him? What would be his song of joy in response?

Explore the Heart of God

- What does it say about the heart of God that in the day David was afraid, he said, "I lay all my fears before you and trust in you with all my heart" (56:3)?

- What did David mean by his question, "What harm could a man bring to me?" (v. 4)? How is this and the trust and praise he voiced in verse 11 connected to the rest of Psalm 56?

- Why is God our soul's "true shelter"? How do you think it looks to "hide beneath the shadow of [God's] embrace, under the wings of [God's] cherubim until this terrible trouble is past" (57:1)?

- What does it say about David's experience of the heart of God that his heart was "quiet and confident" (v. 7)? In what way was this posture connected to his trust and praise?

- In Psalm 59:1-2, David asked God to "protect" him, "keep [him] safe," "put [him] in a high place," and "save" him. What do these requests tell us about what God is capable of and willing to do for us?

- Why is it that David's (and our) strength is found when we "wait upon" the Lord (59:9)? Why could he rely on him? Why would the Lord's strength be David's "song of joy" (v. 16)? Why should we ourselves sing of the Lord's love?

Experience the Heart of God

- When David was afraid, he laid all his fears before the Lord and trusted in him with all his heart. Is this how you typically respond when you're afraid? Why or why not?

- With God on our side, we have no reason to be afraid. After all, "what harm could a man bring to me?" (56:4). How might this attitude of trust deepen our experience of the heart of God over the course of our life?

- "The very moment" David called to the Lord "for a Father's help the tide of battle turns and [his] enemies flee!" (56:9). When have you experienced this aspect of the heart of God yourself?

- Are you experiencing any people or circumstances "like lions just waiting to tear [you] to shreds" (57:4)? How might it look to remain "quiet and confident," as David had? In what way do you want God to protect you, keep you safe, raise you up, and save you? Now ask him, finding strength while waiting for him to act.

• Do you make the Lord's strength your song of joy? How would it impact your experience of the heart of God if you sang with joy the Lord's praises and "the lyrics of [his] faithful love for [you]" (59:17)—especially while you were in trouble?

Share the Heart of God

• Who do you know who is afraid and needs to trust in the Lord with all their heart? How might it look to share the heart of God by sharing with them Psalm 56?

• Why are verses 4–9 such good news for those you know?

• How do you think being "quiet and confident" when trouble comes or people attack can be a powerful way to share the heart of God?

- Wherever you go, do you publicly thank God for his extravagant love and astonishing faithfulness? Why are such acts important to sharing the heart of God?

- Who do you know who needs protection, safety, and salvation? Take time now to ask God to awaken and arise on their behalf.

- David sang the praises of his Strength, Stronghold, and Savior. How might following his lead create opportunities to share the heart of God with those you know?

CONSIDER THIS

David's quietness and confidence during his chaos flowed from the trust and praise he gave to the Lord. When darkness turns its face toward you, may you rise to sing what David sang: "O my Strength, I sing with joy your praises. O my Stronghold, I sing with joy your song! O my Savior, I sing with joy the lyrics of your faithful love for me!" (Psalm 59:17).

Lesson 8

Do You Need a Father's Help?

PSALMS 60, 61, AND 62

For no matter where I am, even when I'm far from home,
I will cry out to you for a Father's help. When I'm feeble
and overwhelmed by life, guide me into your glory
where I am safe and sheltered.
(Psalm 61:2)

The Christian faith is unique for a very important aspect: the way we relate to God. We don't relate to him like other religions have related to their deity through the ages, as a distant and removed Being who is unconcerned with the affairs of the world. No, we relate to him as a *Father*.

While relating to God as Father might be different for you (or even a struggle), consider the kind of care and compassion, provision and protection, safety and salvation an earthly father should provide his child. That's the kind of help that's available to us, which David prayed for numerous times in his experience of oppression and desire for deliverance. He wanted guidance to Father God's safety and shelter, to be lifted high and held firmly.

He recognized God was his only Safe Place, his Champion Defender, his Savior—just as we all long for our earthly fathers to be for us.

God isn't distant and removed, an unblinking Cosmic Stare. He is our ever-present help in times of trouble. He is our Father-Help!

Discover the Heart of God

- After reading Psalms 60, 61, and 62, what did you notice, perhaps for the first time? What questions do you have? What did you learn about the heart of God?

- For David, what did it feel as if God had done to him in Psalm 60?

- What kind of help and trust is worthless and an empty hope? What help do we need instead?

- To what extent did David say he would cry out to God for a Father's help?

- While David waited for the Lord's rescue and salvation in Psalm 62, what did he say he would do?

- Who was David's only Savior and Safe Place, his only Champion Defender? Where shouldn't people put their trust for salvation, safety, and defense?

Explore the Heart of God

- Read Psalm 60:1–3 again. Why do you think God would reject his people like this? Why would God have "taught us hard lessons and made us drink the wine of bewilderment"? What do verses 6–8 tell us about the heart of God—especially in the face of God teaching us hard lessons and seemingly rejecting us?

- Why is it true that "to trust in any man is an empty hope" (v. 11), that human help is worthless?

- Why is it true that none of our foes can touch us when we're "held firmly in [God's] wrap-around presence!"? How is God a "paradise of protection" (61:3)?

- Describe David's posture before God that we find in Psalm 62. What does this say about how David experienced the heart of God?

- Why is it true that "there's no risk of failure with God!" (v. 2)?

Experience the Heart of God

- Have you ever felt that God had walked off and left you, that he had turned against you and deserted you? What was that like?

- Sometimes God needs to teach us "hard lessons" and make us "drink the wine of bewilderment" (60:3). When has God done that with you? How did you experience the heart of God through it?

- David said "to trust in any man is an empty hope" (v. 11). Do you believe this, and does your life reflect this? Why or why not?

- How have you experienced the heart of God as a Father's help? How about as a "paradise of protection," and how has he lifted you "high above the fray" (61:3)?

- When you are troubled, are you shaken and paralyzed with fear? Is God your only Safe Place, Savior, and Champion Defender when it happens? Explain.

- How should Psalm 62:11–12 impact your experience of the heart of God when trouble comes your way?

Share the Heart of God

- For lots of people, it feels as if God has walked off and left them, that he's deserted and turned against them. How might sharing Psalm 60 with them be a way to share the heart of God?

- Who do you know who needs a Father's help to face their "enemies"? Spend some time praying they wouldn't trust in any man but in God. Pray that God will help them "fight like heroes" (v. 12).

- How might Psalm 61 encourage someone you know in their experience of the heart of God in the midst of trouble?

- Sometimes we all need help standing silently and waiting as long as it takes for God to rescue us. How might it look to stand with someone you know while she waits upon the Lord?

- Read Psalm 62:11–12 again. This week, with whom can you share this encouragement straight from the heart of God?

CONSIDER THIS

Do you need a Father's help? Use the prayer Jesus gave us as a guide for asking him for it:

Our Father, dwelling in the heavenly realms,
may the glory of your name
be the center on which our lives turn.
Manifest your kingdom realm,
and cause your every purpose to be fulfilled on earth,
just as it is fulfilled in heaven.
Give us today the bread of tomorrow.
Forgive us the wrongs we have done as we ourselves
release forgiveness to those who have wronged us.
Rescue us every time we face tribulation
and set us free from evil.
For you are the King who rules
with power and glory forever. Amen.
(Matthew 6:9–13)

Lesson 9

God Helps Us like a Father

PSALMS 63, 64, AND 65

You answer our prayers with amazing wonders
and with awe-inspiring displays of power. You are the righteous
God who helps us like a Father. Everyone everywhere looks
to you, for you are the Confidence of all the earth,
even to the farthest islands of the sea.
(Psalm 65:5)

Several years ago, a movie called *Anna and the King* told the story of an English schoolteacher who taught the king of Siam's children. It provides the perfect illustration of what we learn in today's psalms.

At one point in the story, Anna's son got into a fight with the king's son, and the king's youngest daughter ran to her father for help. Casting aside the normal customs for approaching the king, she slammed open the door to the grand palace hall, waded through the throngs of people bowing in respect, trotted up the stairs, and whispered into her father's ear for help. He sprang to his feet and ran down the stairs and through the hall, leaving behind his kingdom business to attend to the pleas of his daughter. She needed father help, and he gave without question.

That's what it's like when we come to God in prayer. He helps us like a father, springing into action to destroy our foes and amaze us with his wonders. God's lovers will be found like this king's children: glad and wrapped in his glorious presence!

Discover the Heart of God

- After reading Psalms 63, 64, and 65, what did you notice, perhaps for the first time? What questions do you have? What did you learn about the heart of God?

- How did David feel toward God in his "weary wilderness" (63:1)? What did David say meant more to him than life itself?

- In Psalm 64, how did David describe the "bands of criminals" from whom he wanted the Lord to keep him safe?

- Why will all "stand awestruck over what God has done" (64:9)? How will the lovers of God respond?

- According to Psalm 65, how does God answer our prayers? How does he help us?

Explore the Heart of God

- In what way might David's lovesickness and cravings for God have been caused by his "weary wilderness" experience?

- What do you think David found in God that he pursued and clung to him with passion (see 63:8)?

- What does it tell us about the heart of God that he "vindicated the victims" of the crimes of the wicked (64:9)?

- What does Psalm 65:1–5 tell us about who God is and our experience of his heart?

- In what way is 65:6–13 connected to David's declaration that "everyone everywhere looks to you, for you are the confidence of all the earth, even to the farthest islands of the sea" (v. 5)?

Experience the Heart of God

- When was the last time you had a "weary wilderness" experience? What was that like? Did it increase your craving and lovesickness for God? Explain.

- Do you agree with David that God's "tender mercies mean more to me than life itself" (63:3)? Why or why not? If so, how do you show it?

- From what "band of criminals" (64:1) are you crying out to the Lord to keep you safe? Spend time now praying for vindication.

- When have you stood "awestruck over what God has done" (v. 9)? Describe that experience.

- Do you agree that God is the God who answers prayers? How often do you come before him with your prayers? Explain.

- How do the signs and wonders of creation as described in Psalm 65:6–13 give you confidence in God's fatherlike help?

Share the Heart of God

- Who do you know who is stuck in a "weary wilderness"? How might sharing the heart of God with them satisfy the cravings only God can fulfill?

- How can you model to others what it means to pursue and cling to God with passion, so they too can experience the heart of God?

- David says of the wicked, "How unsearchable is their endless evil, trying desperately to hide the deep darkness of their hearts" (64:6). How does Psalm 64 encourage those you know who are being attacked by such people?

- This week, with whom can you share a testimony of God's deliverance, so they "stand awestruck over what God has done, seeing how he vindicated the victims of these crimes" (v. 9)?

- Our God is a God of prayer who answers "our prayers with amazing wonders and with awe-inspiring displays of power" (65:5). How can you invite people in your life to come before him with their requests in order to share in the heart of God?

CONSIDER THIS

How are you thirsting, craving, and longing for God and his power and help? What bitter complaints do you have that you need God to hear? Look across the expanse of creation, as Psalm 65 encourages, and see all the ways he is the Confidence of all the earth. May he be your Confidence too, for he is the God who answers prayers!

Lesson 10

Mighty Miracles Have Made Us Who We Are!

PSALMS 66, 67, AND 68

Display your strength, God, and we'll be strong!
For your miracles have made us who we are. Lord, do it again,
and parade from your temple your mighty power.
(Psalm 68:28–29)

The psalms in these lessons are called the Exodus Psalms for a reason: they chronicle experiences of suffering and redemption. Israel had experience with both, particularly redemption. In this lesson we learn something that Israel learned: God's mighty miracles make us who we are!

Take the exodus itself. It is the single defining event in the history of Israel. Yahweh had shown up in their story as the mighty *go'el*, Redeemer. And he displayed his mighty miracle-working power by delivering them from oppressive slavery at the hands of the Egyptians. Then he made a covenant with them to be their God and they his people. To this day the Jewish people still celebrate the Passover, reminding them of this nation-shaping event.

David described such mighty miracle-working power as awe-inspiring, and we should burst forth in praise because of it. And he not only said that God's mighty miracles would shape Israel but that all the world would bow down to worship and sing the glories of God forever for this display of power.

Whether we are fatherless or widows, lonely ones or prisoners, God listens and God acts. When he does, we can't help but be changed!

Discover the Heart of God

- After reading Psalms 66, 67, and 68, what did you notice, perhaps for the first time? What questions do you have? What did you learn about the heart of God?

- What does the psalmist of Psalm 66 want everyone in all the earth to do? Why?

- What are "all the incredible things that God has done" that everyone will say they have to "come and see" (66:5)?

• What was the psalmist's prayer in Psalm 67, and what did he want?

• In 68:5–6, God is described in a number of ways in relationship to his response to certain needy people. List those who are described here.

• Psalm 68 ends with David declaring that God's glory streams from his Holy Place, that he's a God whose power is in heaven and is awesome in his sanctuary. How had the psalmist described this throughout his psalm?

Explore the Heart of God

• In what way is it true that "all the earth will bow down to worship; all the earth will sing your glories forever!" (66:4)?

• What "incredible thing" does the psalmist describe in Psalm 66:6–12 that God did for his people? Why is it so significant and incredible?

• Why did the people of God offer sacrifices to the Lord? Why did the psalmist promise to do so in Psalm 66?

• For what purpose did the psalmist of Psalm 67 want God to bless his people, make his face beam with joy, and send them out over all the earth?

• It's clear the people in Psalm 68 were blessed by the Lord. What was the purpose of that blessing?

- David wrote, "What a glorious God! He gives us salvation over and over, then daily he carries our burdens!" (68:19). In what way was this true for the children of Israel? How is it true for us as well?

Experience the Heart of God

- How might it look in your life to follow the psalmist's direction in Psalm 66:1–4? How can you "lift up your joyful shout to God!" (v. 1)?

- What does it mean to you and your experience of the heart of God that he "holds our lives safely in his hands. He's the One who keeps us faithfully following him" (66:9)?

- In what ways has God kept you "satisfied at his banquet of blessings," and how do "the blessings keep coming" (67:6–7)? List those ways here, then give him the honor he deserves.

• Of the people listed in Psalm 68:5–6, with whom do you identify? Why?

• Psalm 68 tells the story of the way God arose with awesome power for his people. What's your own story with God's power? How have his mighty miracles made you who you are?

Share the Heart of God

• The psalmist directed us to "tell the world how wonderful [God] is" (66:2). What would you say to those you know?

• What incredible things has God accomplished in your life that you would like those you know to "come and see"? How would inviting them to do so help them share in God's heart, and how can you help them?

- The psalmist asked God to "send us out all over the world so that everyone everywhere will discover your ways and know who you are and see your power to save!" (67:2). How can you go forth and share the heart of God in such a way that those you know discover and know God's ways and saving power?

- In 68:5–6, David described God in a number of ways. Which of these descriptions specifically apply to someone you know in need? How can you share the hope of Psalm 68 in order to share the heart of God?

- David declared, "What a glorious God! He gives us salvation over and over, then daily he carries our burdens!" (v. 19). Why is this such good news to those you know who need to share in the heart of God?

CONSIDER THIS

How have God's mighty miracles shaped you, just like the exodus shaped the Jewish people? Ultimately, God's mighty miracle-working power on the cross has made you who you are: a forgiven, guilt-free child of God! Now do what David encouraged: give it up for God and proclaim his majesty for making you who you are through his mighty miracle-working power!

Lesson 11

———

God, Don't Delay: Come Quickly!

PSALMS 69 AND 70

Lord, in my place of weakness and need,
won't you turn your heart toward me and hurry to help me?
For you are my Savior and I'm always in your thoughts.
So don't delay to deliver me now, for you are my God.
(Psalm 70:5)

Have you ever felt like you're nearly drowning in a flood, the waters rising higher and higher to your neck; or you're sinking deep into mud with no place to stand; you're tired and worn out; your throat is hoarse and your eyes are swollen from crying; people are against you; you're weak and needy. And all the while waiting for the Lord to act. To do something. Anything!

Sometimes it seems as if God is far away when we need him most. But what David reminds us in this lesson is that "God does listen to the poor and needy and will not abandon his prisoners of love" (Psalm 69:33). Despite all of what David experienced above, he knew God was there and was not silent. So he cried out to him and demanded that he come—and come quickly! The reason he did is because he knew God would bend down and listen, and his answer would be his sure salvation.

This lesson reminds us that no matter what's happening, we can do and know the same.

Discover the Heart of God

- After reading Psalm 69 and 70, what did you notice, perhaps for the first time? What questions do you have? What did you learn about the heart of God?

- In Psalm 69, David said he needed saving. What imagery did he use to describe his situation?

- How did David put his requests to God for help in verses 13–18? How did he want his enemies treated in verses 22–28?

- What did David promise God would do for his gentle lovers, for the poor and needy?

• Describe David's cry for help in Psalm 70. How did David describe who he was and his place of trouble?

Explore the Heart of God

• What does it say in Psalm 69 about David's troubles that they were like rising flood waters, that he was sinking into mud, that he was about to drown in a storm, and that his throat was dry and his voice was gone (vv. 1-2)? What does it say about David's relationship with the Lord that he was "waiting for ... God to come through" for him in the midst of such trouble (v. 3)?

• What do you think David meant that he wanted the Lord to keep him "from ever being a stumbling block to others, to those who love [God]" (v. 6)?

- Read Psalm 69:13-18 again. What does it reveal to us about prayer and the heart of God? How should Psalm 70:4 shape our response to God in prayer?

- What does Psalm 69:19-28 tell us about those who do us wrong and the heart of God?

- David tells us, "God does listen to the poor and needy and will not abandon his prisoners of love. ... God will come to save his Zion-people" (vv. 33, 35). What does this tell us about the heart of God?

- What does it say about our own cries for help that David prayed to the Lord, "Come quickly and rescue me! ... Don't delay to deliver me now. For you are my God" (70:1, 5)?

Experience the Heart of God

- Have you ever felt like David in Psalm 69:1–3? That the flood waters of your troubles were up to your neck? What was that like?

- In what ways do you need to see the Lord's tender kindness, his grace, his compassion, and his constant love (v. 16)? Spend time telling him what you need, trusting he will answer.

- How does it make you feel to know that "God does listen to the poor and needy and will not abandon his prisoners of love. ... God will come to save his Zion-people" (vv. 33, 35)?

- In what ways do you need the Lord to "come quickly and rescue me!" (70:1)? List them here, then post them somewhere to remind you of the ways God will come through for you.

- Do you continually rejoice in your Savior, saying aloud, "How great and glorious is our God!" (v. 4)? Why or why not?

Share the Heart of God

- Who do you know who feels as David did in Psalm 69:1–3? How can you share the heart of God with them this week? Spend a moment praying for them, that God would come through for them.

- Do you know anyone who has been mocked, cursed, and disgraced for their love of the Lord? How can you encourage them to not let anything turn their zeal away?

• How might Psalm 69:22–28 encourage someone you know who is being attacked by people? How might sharing 69:32–36 with them help them share in the heart of God?

• Who in your life needs God to come quickly to rescue and restore them? Pray now for such quick favor.

CONSIDER THIS

David knew for certain that God's miracle rescue would eventually come to him, lifting him to a higher place; that God would come and save his people; that his people would eventually overflow with gladness because of God's rescue; and that God's lovers would live in peace and safety. May you know the same. And may you erupt with excitement and joy when he comes and does what he's promised!

Lesson 12

———

Cry Out for a Father's Compassion!

PSALMS 71 AND 72

O King of kings, they will all bow before you.
O King of kings, every nation will one day serve you.
He will care for the needy and neglected when they cry to
him for help. The humble and helpless will know his kindness, for
with a father's compassion he will save their souls.
(Psalm 72:11–1)

As he did with the cries of oppression that stretched out of the sun-drenched sands of Egypt and made their way up the stairways to the highest heavens, God continues to hear and he continues to act. This was true in the book of Exodus, it has been true in our Exodus Psalms, and it will be true in the book of your own life.

In our final lesson on suffering and redemption, David reveals several truths that we need to carry with us and hold onto tightly. Yes, the Lord is our shelter and place of safety; he is our protection and provider. But he's more than that. He is *with* us, and has been since the day we were born! He also stays with us when we're old and gray. As he did with his people in Egypt, God will hear the cries of the needy and neglected, and he will offer them help. With a father's compassion he will save them!

That's the hope of Exodus and the promise of the Exodus Psalms. Though we may sink down with trials and troubles, the Lord will revive us again, freeing us from oppression and lifting us out of the pit of death.

Discover the Heart of God

- After reading Psalms 71 and 72, what did you notice, perhaps for the first time? What questions do you have? What did you learn about the heart of God?

- In whom had David taken refuge, and who was his shelter? What did David seek in response?

- How long had David hung on to the Lord? Now that he was old, what didn't David want?

- How had David's enemies attacked him, and what had they said about him? What did he want God to do to them in response?

- Even though God had let David "sink down with trials and troubles" (71:20), what was David certain God would do? How did he say he'd respond?

- What had Solomon asked of God? What did he want him to give the king? How had Solomon described the kind of rule he hoped God would give the king? What did Solomon want the poor and needy to have with the king? Describe what he would do.

Explore the Heart of God

- Psalm 71 says David had taken refuge and found his shelter in the Lord. Why do you think he said to God, "Don't ever let me down!" (v. 1)? Does that strike you as a bit audacious?

• What does it tell us about the heart of God that "no matter what," David would "trust in [the Lord] to help me. Nothing will stop me from praising you to magnify your glory!" (v. 14)?

• Read verses 5–9 again. What does this tell us about the extent of God's care for our lives?

• What does it tell us about the heart of God that the king would want the Lord to give him a heart of justice?

• How is Psalm 72 overall connected to Solomon's request in verses 1–2?

Experience the Heart of God

- How has the Lord been your secure shelter? Has he ever let you down?

- In what ways have you witnessed the revelation-truth that the Lord supported you from the day you were born?

- In what ways do you echo David's plea, "O God, stay close to me! Don't just watch from a distance! Hurry to help me, my God!" (71:12)?

- In response to God's faithful heart toward him, David said that "the harp in my heart will praise your melodies" (v. 22). How do you praise God for his faithfulness? Now take time to do that now.

- How would you like God's justice to be executed on earth? Pray for that now, that the "poor and humble [would] have an advocate with the king," that God would "consider the children of the poor and crush the cruel oppressor" (72:4).

Share the Heart of God

- Who do you know who needs to find their secure shelter in the Lord? How can you share with them the heart of the God who never lets us down?

- Spend time praying for this person you know, that God would stay close to them and not just watch from a distance, but hurry to help.

- David speaks what's true of us all: "I couldn't begin to count the times you've been there for me" (71:15). How might it look to testify about God's faithfulness to those you know as a way to share the heart of God?

- Psalm 72 speaks of a nation being dependent on the righteousness of its "king." Pray for your own leaders, that God would make them godly "judges" and help them "give true justice to [his] people" (72:2).

CONSIDER THIS

May we join Solomon in singing of the One who has redeemed and delivered us from oppression and suffering: "Praise forever Jehovah God, the God of Israel! He is the one and only God of wonders, surpassing every expectation. The blazing glory of his name will be praised forever! May all the earth overflow with his glory! Faithful is our King! Amen!" (Psalm 72:18–19).